fifty
creative
ways to use
paperbacks
in the primary
grades

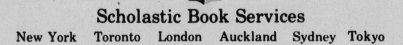

Scholastic Book Services
New York   Toronto   London   Auckland   Sydney   Tokyo

See-Saw is Scholastic's paperback book club for kindergarten and first grade. *Lucky* is Scholastic's paperback book club for second and third grades.

Compiled by Anita Dutt

Illustrations by Bill Cummings

ISBN 0-590-31848-9

12 11 10 9 8 7 6 5 4 3 2 1   9   0 1 2 3 4 5/8
Printed in the U.S.A.   07

Ann S. Richards *11 - 1980*

Contents

Introduction

"It's Like Christmas Every Month!"

"It's just like Christmas! We tear open the carton and hand out the books. Then we all start talking about them and make promises to swap. And then we read. . . . It's like Christmas every month!"

This was Willie's report of the paperback book club in his school. He spoke with the pride of a veteran football player telling about his team. Reading had become his sport, and he was bragging about it.

As I learned to know Willie better and got on his book-swap list, I realized that this youngster had been won over by the same strategy Daniel Fader prescribed in his best-selling paperback, *Hooked on Books.*

In that remarkable book, first published in 1968, Dr. Fader told of transforming non-reading children into enthusiastic readers. His initial experiment, since duplicated in countless situations, set up three basic guidelines:

1. Provide a wide variety of paperbacks for children to choose from.
2. Let each child decide which book he or she will read.
3. See that the child becomes the owner of the book selected.

Daniel Fader escorted the children in his experiment to the biggest book jobber in Detroit and turned them loose to pick their paperbacks. Those children used shopping carts to transport their choices. Given freedom to choose and time to read what they had chosen, the children were quite literally "hooked on books."

The Paperback Book Club Plan

The paperback book club plan, now operating in close to half of the elementary schools in the English-speaking world, began more than 20 years before Fader's Hooked-on-Books project. A book club does not take every child to a paperback warehouse in order to select books. It does bring an intriguing and colorful monthly list to each child right in the classroom where selections are made and orders recorded.

Then, when the carton of books arrives, "It's like Christmas," as Willie put it.

But You Have to Plan for Christmas

What Willie didn't realize was that his excitement over the arrival of the paperback order was due in large measure to the enthusiasm and ingenuity of his classroom teacher. Like Christmas, a book club needs a creative plan to keep the lights sparkling.

Today's children are looking for more than efficient checking and distribution of books. Long hours of TV viewing have taught them to demand diversity, excitement, and emotional pull. These children need a special kind of encouragement and stimulation if their Book Day is to be "just like Christmas."

A Sparkle that Is Contagious

Teaching children to read — and to enjoy reading —is a new kind of ball game today. The old question of "phonics now or later" pales beside the question of how to interest modern youngsters in books and reading. We can't assume that children want to read or even that they have handled appealing books. For many, reading is an unfamiliar experience. They haven't seen their parents reading, perhaps, so they do not see reading as something to strive for or give their time and effort to.

This is the new challenge teachers face.

Every individual — child or adult — does better the thing he wants to do well. The desire to succeed springs from assurance that it will pay off in pleasure and satisfaction.

Today's children have to learn from experience that reading can create delight too good to miss, that books can bring them closer to their friends and open doors to new and exciting ideas and heartwarming experiences. The sooner a child achieves this positive assurance, the easier it will be for him or her to learn to read, to think, and to live creatively.

But how does a teacher introduce books so that both children and reading flourish? How do other teachers do it?

The Scholastic paperback book clubs for children asked this very question of classroom teachers. The answers poured in from Canada, Australia, and the United States — fresh, innovative, and classroom-tested.

This book is a round-up of teachers' reports on how they have developed the paperback book club plan so as to make reading a vital and rewarding part of every child's life.

There are suggestions for setting up a book nook and reading activity center; for board games and puzzles that can be made from next to nothing; for posters, bulletin boards, and murals that promote books and reading; for getting parents involved; and for end-of-the-year happenings.

Not one proposal requires spending large sums of money for materials. And not one will take a great deal of time to set up and launch.

Like a breath of fresh air on a muggy day, each of these ideas come in with a sparkle that is contagious.

— Nancy Larrick

Nancy Larrick, a founder and former president of the International Reading Association, is widely known for her books and articles on children and their education. She is the author of A Parent's Guide to Children's Reading *and* A Teacher's Guide to Children's Books, *and the editor of twelve anthologies of poetry. For a number of years, Dr. Larrick directed the Poetry Workshop for Teachers at Lehigh University.*

It's Book Day

Enthusiasm reaches a peak on the day the books arrive in the classroom. Teachers often distribute the books then and there. But sometimes a special activity makes reading a celebration, as in the two ideas that follow.

Our lucky day

When the books arrive, place them all on a table with the child's *Lucky* or *See-Saw News* coupon or his name clipped to the cover of the child's book(s). If you have ordered dividend copies for the class library, label them "our library."

This display gives girls and boys a chance to look over the many kinds of books the class has ordered from their book club — a sure way to stir up reading interest.

At a given time, children put their work away and get ready for "book-club time." Those who have ordered books now go to the table and pick them up.

Children who have not ordered books may choose one of the free dividend books the teacher has selected from the club list. Then everyone (including the teacher) finds a place to relax and read — at desks, seated on carpet squares on the floor, at (or under) tables, etc.

After half an hour or so, invite any children who wish to do so to tell their classmates about their new books.

To limit interruptions during this special time, one third-grade teacher places a sign on the classroom door: THIS IS OUR LUCKY DAY. DO NOT DISTURB.

A paperback treasure hunt

This favorite activity of book-club sponsors depends on a secret delivery of the books. If your book box is automatically sent to your room, you may want to arrange to have it held in the office until you can pick it up secretly.

After the class has gone, separate the books into several stacks and hide the stacks around the room. When the children come back the next day (or after lunch), divide them into two teams. Give each team a different starting clue written on a piece of paper (to be read aloud to the youngest primary graders) and turn them loose.

One clue leads to another (all planted by you, of course), until all the books are found. Even children who have not ordered a book share in the excitement.

All Kinds of Books

Sometimes children concentrate all their reading on a single area of interest. Nothing is wrong with this up to a point, but you may want to try one of the following activities to make young readers aware of the variety of books available to them.

Reading wheel

One primary-grade teacher gets her class rolling with a colorful reading wheel.

Draw a large circle (about two feet across) on construction paper or cardboard, and cut it out. Divide the circle into wedges for reading categories and label these sections — Fiction, Science, Crafts, and so on.

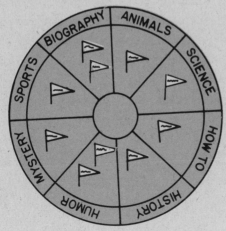

Enid Bjarnson writes, "I make little flags of white paper and round toothpicks with a pin taped to the end to hold it to the wheel."

The children write the titles of books they have read on these flags, and pin the flags to the wheel in the category they think is right for the book.

Almost any See-Saw or Lucky listing will provide the variety of subjects needed to make this project successful.

Aim for variety

A second-grade teacher individualizes a similar activity.

Each child keeps a "Reading Record Folder" with the book titles listed on one page and a bull's-eye pattern on the facing page. The bull's-eye is divided into six or eight categories, such as Sports, Animals, Mystery, Biography, and so on. Three or four circles are drawn into each section.

The child colors in a circle for every book completed in one of the categories.

Their teacher, Gail Greenberg, writes: "I find the category concept very beneficial . . . Many times a child is interested only in animal stories. But filling in the bull's-eye stimulates interest in other subjects."

When a bull's-eye is filled in, the child gets a prize. But the true reward has been in the reading!

A rainbow of reading

A busy classroom library is a successful one, but it may be hard for children to find the books they want. This categorizing scheme will help children locate books they want and return them to the proper place. It also gives you a good place to house your paperback collection.

First, sort your classroom books according to categories.

Collect cardboard boxes — cereal boxes, soap boxes, and cartons of various sizes from the supermarket. Use an Exacto knife to cut out part of one side panel and the top from each box to make standing bookcases.

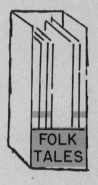

The next step is to color-code the boxes according to the categories you have prepared. Enlist a teacher's aide or some students to help out.

Color-code the boxes with magic markers or crayons on long strips of masking tape; label the boxes as shown.

Cut smaller two-inch strips of the same color to tape to the books in that group. Tape these pieces at the bottom of each book's spine. Now your books are ready to put in their matching cartons.

Since Caroline Levine began using this scheme, her class has been borrowing up to 60 books a week!

Feature of the month

In order to spur interest in books, Lois Martin inaugurated a "feature of the month." Here's how it works.

Ms. Martin groups her classroom library by interest areas, then features one area each month.

"During non-fiction month, the children read on a great variety of subjects, from ants to weather. New doors are opened to them and their interest in reading increases.

"Fantasy month brings delightful challenges and a waiting line for the above-grade-level books, which they check out to read at home. Even slow readers want to check out the *Oz* books, *Mary Poppins*, and *Gulliver's Stories*."

You can encourage young readers to be "book critics" by asking them to express their opinions on a checklist of titles. Pass out a dittoed checklist at the beginning of the month and ask the children to draw a smiley face if they liked a book, a frowning face if they didn't.

A mix of reading levels each month provides reading for everyone and a challenge as well. Ms. Martin writes, "By collecting the forms at the end of the month, I can judge how widely each child is reading and see which books are favorites." The only requirement should be that everyone read at least one book each month.

> Display the books in a dish drainer — an ideal holder for paperbacks of all sizes.

More than a Bulletin Board

Bulletin board displays that invite class participation are featured in this section.

Bulletin board library

To motivate your children to read books, or to spotlight certain paperbacks, put up a bulletin board library.

Construction paper or a piece of fabric makes an attractive background for this display.

Tie a piece of colorful yarn or string lengthwise through each book, with yarn to spare at the top. Loop this yarn around push pins on the bulletin board. With a headline and perhaps a few appropriate decorations, your display is ready.

Avoid a bare bulletin board when the books are out being read by making a back-up for each book displayed — a rectangle of colored paper with the title and author printed on it.

Author: _____

Title: _____

It's a great book because

_____
_____
_____

Name _____

Class _____

A reading tree

The bulletin board can be used to share information about books.

Make a large tree out of construction paper or painted cardboard. Make a suitable label for the trunk, such as, "Pick a paperback from the reading tree."

Cut a supply of apples from red construction paper and mark them (as shown) with spaces big enough for your students to write in. Younger children will need bigger apples.

As children read books they particularly enjoy, they fill in an apple card and pin it to the tree. "One by one the apples grow on the tree, while the paperback books disappear off the rack. This project has encouraged many of my students to read more books, and has helped others find books they might enjoy reading," writes Paulette O'Doherty. "Try it!"

Touchdown with reading

The sports theme makes this an appealing activity and display.

Map out a football field on a bulletin board. The dimensions can be any size that suits your room.

Divide the field at "10-yard" intervals, as shown in the illustration, and label goalposts at each end.

Next divide the class into two teams. Each child gets a paper cut-out player to move when the action starts.

For every book that a child reads and reports on, the team gets to move one of its players toward the goal post, "10 yards" at a time. The first team with all its members behind the goalpost wins.

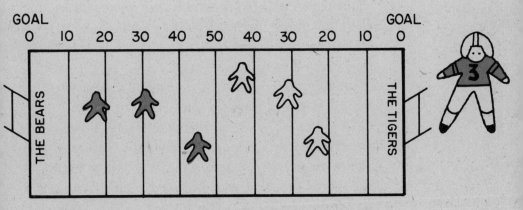

HERMAN FLIES IN A BASKET

HERMAN PAINTS A PICTURE

HERMAN GETS HIS OWN HOUSE

Story-telling mural

"I have a long bulletin board in the hallway that needs some creative ideas once in a while," writes Susan Anderson.

For ideas Ms. Anderson turns to her classroom collection of Lucky books. "I read one of the longer books to my second-graders (one with lots of action, such as *Herman the Great*), and we talk about all the events," Ms. Anderson explains.

Then, with the class's help, Ms. Anderson lists the events in sequence on the chalkboard. Each child picks one event to illustrate. The child may draw, paint, or make a collage.

"We put up all the pictures in order on the long bulletin board," Ms. Anderson continues. She adds the finishing touch — a caption for each picture — and the story mural is complete.

"It's great!" Ms. Anderson says. "My kids can retell the story for other children, and you often

HERMAN RIDES HIS MODEL CAR.

HERMAN FLIES TO NEW YORK AND LANDS IN CENTRAL PARK

see children in the hall reading the story as they go by." And, she writes, "The mural encourages children to read the book themselves."

Poster delight

Many teachers decorate the reading corner or a classroom wall with large poster drawings of book covers. You'll find they have the same instant effect as travel posters in an airline office!

Beverly Clayton's class makes posters based on actual book covers, adding personal touches with collage, paints, or other materials.

"These pictures really interest the other students. The paperbacks illustrated on posters are the ones most read by the whole class."

The Book Nook

Children appreciate having a place to read alone, such as a carpeted corner with a few chairs set aside from the rest of the classroom. Design a book nook for your class based on one of the following ideas.

Favorite-book room divider

The whole class can get involved in making a decorative screen to use as a room divider.

You will need a large cardboard box from a furniture or appliance store — a refrigerator carton is ideal, or you may use a mattress box. Cut the carton down one side and cut off the end flaps. Now it should be about six feet high, ten to twelve feet long.

Most of these boxes are creased lengthwise in two or four places. They can be bent back at these places to enable the screen to stand freely.

Use a measuring tape to divide the screen into as many rectangles as there are children.

Each child will use a rectangle to illustrate a favorite book — a picture that is a personal creation or one based on the actual book cover.

The third-grade teacher who originated this idea has a planning session with the class; she suggests that they draw one or two simple objects for each book, such as an airplane to illustrate *The Wright Brothers,* or a spider for *Charlotte's Web.*

Tempera paint or felt-tip markers are good if the children will be working directly on the cardboard panels. Working at the screen in small groups is advisable.

Another approach is to give each child a piece of drawing paper that will fit the panels. Schedule a paint-in and, later, paste the pictures onto the screen.

Encourage the class to use bright colors and fill in the whole space. They should print the book title in black magic marker, then sign their own names.

Now place your screen so that it divides a reading corner from the rest of the room. A rug and cushions will make the corner inviting.

Have an inaugural session (refreshments optional!) to give everyone a chance to enjoy the artwork. Try to have at least one copy of each child's favorite book on hand.

Under the reading umbrella

Set up a bright beach umbrella to create a reading corner. Use a few plastic pails to hold an assortment of choice paperbacks. With one or two rugs or cushions on the floor, a cheerful reading area is ready.

On your own

Many teachers combine the quiet-reading corner with the classroom library, adding a bookshelf or spin-rack. Children can browse and discover books with a real sense of independence.

The reading corner can also be the class's activity center.

An Activity Center

This section gives some activities that can help beginning readers learn how to get the most pleasure and information from books.

Matchbox books

Amy Zehm, a special education teacher, creates enchanting little matchbox books by cutting the book covers from the book club list and mounting them on empty matchboxes. For larger covers, she uses paperclip boxes.

Inside each little "book" she puts a folded-up slip of paper on which she's written an activity suggestion relating to the book. (For a Clifford book she might write, "Make a picture of Clifford, or of your own dog.")

Children who read a Lucky book have the fun of picking out the corresponding matchbox book, opening the drawer, and finding an activity to do. "Change the activity slips from time to time," Ms. Zehm suggests. "And, of course, make new matchbox books each time you receive a new book club list."

"Go fish" — activity cards

Presented with all the books in a classroom library, some children just don't know what to read. Catch their interest with a basket of books and matching activity cards.

After ordering the children's books and some free books, one second-grade teacher cuts the miniature book covers from the book poster that is part of most book-club offers.

She pastes the cover onto a card (3½" x 8½") and prints the title next to it. Below this she suggests an open-ended activity, such as,"Write your favorite recipe." Or she may give a simple motivation such as a riddle about the book.

The child goes to the book basket, pulls out a card at random, and is drawn to a book that he might otherwise overlook.

A variation of this idea gives an excellent way of keeping track of borrowed books. Make a card for each book, with the mini-cover and title and spaces for borrowers to write in their names.

Date	Borrowed by

Children's own ideas

One teacher encourages the children to make their own activity cards. She "sells" a few books that she has ordered earlier from the club. Then children sign up to read them in the classroom library.

They write two or three questions that can be answered easily by reading the book, and an activity that can be done with the book.

She cuts out the synopsis of the book from the book club News and pastes it onto a 5″ x 8″ card, along with the children's questions. Each child is credited for his part on the card.

Games from Scratch

Games you can make yourself, from ordinary classroom materials, help motivate reading and reinforce basic skills.

A matching game

Carolyn London, a second-grade teacher, uses the *Lucky News* for many independent and group activities, including a matching game that is a favorite with her children. This is how the game works.

Take an extra copy of the *Lucky News* and cut it apart to separate the pictures of the book covers and the blurbs (summaries).

Cut colored construction paper into 4½″ x 3½″ pieces. Mount the book covers on some pieces and the blurbs on others. If the blurb refers to the book by name, delete the name and substitute a pronoun.

Code the matching cards with matching symbols, numbers, or letters on the back. Then make packets of 12 matching blurbs and titles.

"Children use the packets individually, self-checking, or use them in pairs, and time each other," Ms. London explains. "This has proved to be a popular game with my students."

In addition to being fun, this matching game helps improve reading comprehension.

A relay race

"We always read the book club *News* thoroughly," Judy Jones writes. "All children are eager to get a turn to read the description of one of the books."

After the book descriptions are read and discussed, Mrs. Jones divides the class into two teams for a book club news relay game. She calls out the title of a book and asks a team to find the name of the author, or the number of pages, or some other fact given in the *News*. Then it is the next team's turn and so on for as long as interest remains.

This game gives children good practice in scanning for specific information.

"Word Cubes" — an alphabetizing game

"To help teach my pupils library skills — particularly in locating books — I have been saving the miniature pictures of Lucky books featured in the *Teachers' Guide*," writes Jean Swenson, a third-grade teacher.

Mrs. Swenson uses the miniature book covers and 5″ x 8″ index cards to make playing pieces for an alphabetizing game she calls "Word Cubes." First Mrs. Swenson makes a pattern for the cubes, marking off six sections, each 1½″ square (see illustration). By drawing the pattern on a duplicating master, she can run off many at one time. The pattern is printed on the unlined sides of the index cards.

After the patterns are printed on the index cards, cut them out. Then glue on the miniature book covers — one cover to each section for a total of six covers per cube. (It will be necessary to cut some of the miniature covers to fit in the squares, but be sure the title and author's name remain intact.)

Now fold the longer section into a cube shape and glue the two end flaps together. Fold up the short section, tuck the two side flaps in, and the cube is complete

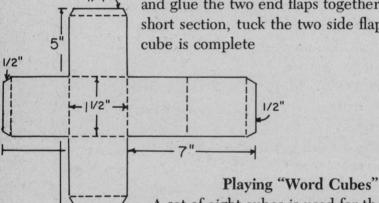

Playing "Word Cubes"

A set of eight cubes is used for the game. (You may want to make several sets to accommodate several groups of children.)

You also need to make two answer keys for each set. Answer Key #1 is an alphabetical listing of all *titles* used in the set; Answer Key #2 is an alphabetical listing of all *authors*.

Two to four children may play at once. The children decide if they want to play "Title Word Cubes" or "Author Word Cubes," depending on whether they feel like alphabetizing by titles or by authors.

The first player chooses five cubes. He tosses them like dice, one at a time, in front of him. Looking at the book covers that are on top, the child arranges the five covers in alphabetical order — by title or by author, whichever has been decided.

Another child in the group checks the player's arrangement, consulting the appropriate answer key. If the player is correct, he gets five points. If not, he receives no points. The first player to reach 50 points (or whatever number the children agree on) is declared the winner.

"Some children like to use the sets of cubes individually and then check themselves just for fun," Mrs. Swenson writes. "The game is a marvelous incentive for children to learn alphabetizing skills as well as better use of the library."

Your girls and boys will probably think up other games to play with these appealing (and sturdy) little cubes. How about "Toss the Cube" to decide which Lucky book to read next!

A board game for beginning readers

This simple board game uses extra copies of the children's *Lucky* or *See-Saw Book Club News* and the mini-book poster featured each month in the *Teachers' Guide*.

To make the game, you need a large poster-board. Mark out a winding path of squares on the board and label one end START and the other FINISH.

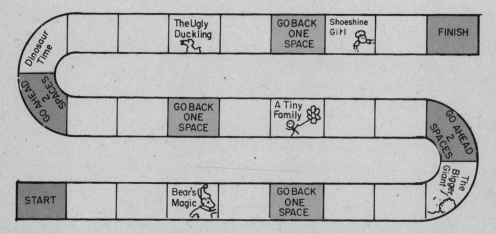

Take two extra copies of the children's *Lucky* or *See-Saw News* and cut out the pictures of the book covers (you will not need the descriptions). Where no picture is shown, cut out the title and the author's name. Secure the pictures of the book covers and titles to random squares on the path. In some of the other squares, letter in directions such as "Go ahead 2 spaces" — to add to the excitement.

30

Next, detach from the *Lucky* or *See-Saw Teachers' Guide* the book poster showing book covers in color. Cut the poster apart and glue each little book cover to a small square of cardboard or an index card. Then get another dozen blank cards and mark each with a number: 1, 2, or 3. Put the two sets of cards together and mix well.

Use buttons or pebbles as markers.

Playing the game

Place the shuffled cards facedown in a pile.

The first player picks the top card. If it is a number, he moves his marker the required number of spaces. If it is a book cover, he reads the title and looks over the board to find the matching cover. He moves his marker directly to the square bearing the matching cover.

The game continues. Whenever a child draws a book-cover card, he must move to the corresponding book cover (or title) on the board — even if it means going backwards.

Any child who cannot read the title of a book he has drawn is penalized: he must go back two squares.

After a player moves, he replaces the card facedown on the bottom of the pile. The first child to reach FINISH is the winner. The game may continue until all players cross the finish line.

"What am I?"

"Children enjoy games, and this one can be a real learning experience in reading and comprehension," writes Joyce Dahlquist, a third-grade teacher.

"After distributing the *Lucky News*, ask the children to read carefully, for they are going to play a game using the information about the books."

While the girls and boys are reading and talking about the books, pin the small picture of a book taken from the Lucky book poster or just the book name to the back of each child. Use only titles on the current order form even if some must be used twice.

"Since children cannot see which book is on their own back," Ms. Dahlquist continues, "they must ask questions to find out."

The questions, based on information in the *Lucky News*, should be ones that can be answered yes or no. (For example, *Does my book have 64 pages? Is it about a real person?*)

To add to the fun, Ms. Dahlquist gives away one or two free books at the end of the game. The teacher draws the winners from a box containing the names of all the children who guessed their book title.

Concentration

"Very few kindergarten children know how to read, but one of the best things I can do to create a desire to read in my youngsters is to create a love of stories," writes Fern Thompson. She finds this game of Concentration effective.

Making the cards

Save a few copies of the student *See-Saw News* to make a deck of playing cards.

Cut out two identical pictures of the books and mount them on small cards, approximately 3″ x 3″.

Cover the face of each card with clear plastic or Contac paper, then cover the back of each card with a piece of patterned Contac paper. By using a different pattern for each deck, you can have more than one deck in use at the same time. Ms. Thompson usually has 40 to 50 pairs in one deck.

Playing the game (2–4 players)

The cards are mixed and turned facedown on a table. Each child in turn chooses two cards and turns them faceup for all to see. The cards must stay in place throughout play of the game.

If the child turns up two identical cards, he gets to keep them and take another turn. He can play as long as he can turn up matching cards.

If the pair of cards does not match, they are turned facedown again and the play goes on to the next child. The game ends when all cards have been won. Whoever has the most pairs is the winner.

Ms. Thompson adds, "I read aloud each book that is used in the game so the stories are familiar. The children usually discuss the books and call them by name as they turn up the cards."

Paperback Challenge

This board game encourages children to read paperbacks on their own. Phyllis O'Sullivan devised rules to help her students develop good listening skills and interpretive skills.

Making the game

The board: On a piece of construction paper, draw an oval racetrack divided into 20 or so squares. Label one square START and the square directly to its left FINISH. Cut out the little book covers featured in the *Teachers' Guide* and glue or tape one in each remaining square of the track.

Number cards: Make a set of cards with the numbers 1, 2, and 3. (Or make a spinner with these numbers.)

Story cards: Use index cards or pieces of oaktag cut to index-card size. On each card, glue or tape a book description clipped from the *Lucky News*. (Do not include the title or author.) Use only descriptions of books whose covers are shown on the track.

Place the number cards in a bag or box and the playing cards in a separate pile.

Playing the game

Two players work together as a team (four players in all). Each player has a cardboard race car, a button, or some other marker.

The first player picks a number card and moves his marker the number of spaces indicated. He reads aloud the title of the book he has landed on. Then he goes through the pile of story cards, selects one, and reads it aloud. He then challenges

the opposing team, "Does this story match this book cover?" (The player may try to trick his opponents by purposely choosing a card that does *not* match.)

If the opposing team replies correctly, one of them may take a turn. But if the answer is wrong, the first team goes again. (Team members take turns.) The first player who reaches the finish square wins for his team.

If the children want to play a longer game, they may require both members of a team to finish in order to win.

Lucky Book Look Game

"My class really loves this game, and it is a good way to get them interested in reading for fun," writes Rebecca Mallet, a second-grade teacher.

The Lucky Book Look Game is a combination of Bingo and Concentration. The game cards are made from Lucky Book Club materials.

Here's what you need to make your own Lucky Book Look Game, which can be played by two, three, or four children.

Gameboards (make 4)

Each gameboard should have nine different books (36 covers needed for the four gameboards).

Tagboard, 7" x 10" divided into nine sections, each 2⅜" x 2¾". In each section, glue a book cover cut from the Book Notes section of the *Lucky Teachers' Guide.*

Playing cards (make 36)

Cut 5″ x 8″ index cards into eight little cards, each 2″ x 2½″. (You will need 36 little cards in all.)

Then get extra copies of the children's *Lucky News;* clip out the title and author for each book used on the gameboards. Glue one clipping onto each little card. (If you don't have extra copies of the *News,* print the titles and authors on the cards.)

Turn the cards over and print the words "Book Look" on each.

You may want to laminate all the game cards to make them more durable.

Put the game cards in a large manila envelope and list the rules on the outside.

How to play the Lucky Book Look Game

1. Shuffle the playing cards and place them face down in straight rows between the players.

2. The first player chooses a card, turns it over, and reads the title and author. If the title matches a book picture on his gameboard, he may cover that picture with the playing card. If not, he must put the card back, face down.

3. You should watch for cards that you need and remember where they are when it's your turn.

4. The first player to get 3 in a row — across, down, or diagonally — wins. Or play "Blackout" — cover all the book pictures to win.

The Magic Box

To get first-grade children interested in reading books, try playing this simple game.

One child puts his favorite paperback into the Magic Box, without letting the other children see the book. Then the child comes to the front of the room. It's up to the other children to guess what book is in the box by asking questions that can be answered yes or no — questions about characters, plot, setting, and the like.

The child whose book is in the box can answer only yes or no to the questions.

Everybody wins

Here is an individual event for beginning readers. Use free dividend books as prizes.

Each week, set aside special time for quiet reading. When a child finishes a book, you may wish to have a conversation with him about the book.

Every child who completes 10 books gets to pick a paperback to keep for his very own. Then he may start on the second lap of his "race."

Everybody wins this game!

Around the World with Books

This game combines listening skills and comprehension skills. The procedure is based on an old game called "Around the World."

Read a chapter or several pages of a book every day to the class. When the book is completed, ask a number of questions — questions on plot, characters, vocabulary, and so on — which you have jotted down on index cards. (The answers can be put on the backs of the cards.)

Student number one stands next to student two, and you ask both a question. The one who responds first with the correct answer wins and moves over to student number three. The loser takes his seat again.

A winner is always moving around the classroom or around the world!

Children are eager to play this game. Their enthusiasm often motivates them to read along in their own copies of the paperback the teacher is reading in class.

More Fun and Games – puzzles, mostly

Lucky word-hunt game

Mary Murphy's second-graders have the fun of being puzzle-makers as well as puzzle-solvers and book-readers when she invites them to make their own Lucky word-hunt games.

After reading a book from the "Lucky Book Corner," a child is given a paper with a mimeographed grid — 15 half-inch squares by 8 squares (120 squares total) — made by the teacher.

To the right of the grid is space for a list of 12 words. Below is room for the child to draw a picture representing the book.

To make a puzzle, the child chooses 12 pertinent words from the Lucky book he has read and lists them in the appropriate space next to the grid. Then the child writes the words, one letter per square, in different places on the grid (some vertically, some horizontally). Finally he fills in all the blank squares with letters, thus "hiding" the 12 words.

After the child draws a simple illustration, Ms. Murphy copies the puzzle on a ditto master and runs off copies for the whole class. Children never tire of the game, circling the hidden words on each classmate's puzzle. The activity has another positive effect: it keeps them reading and enjoying their Lucky book collection.

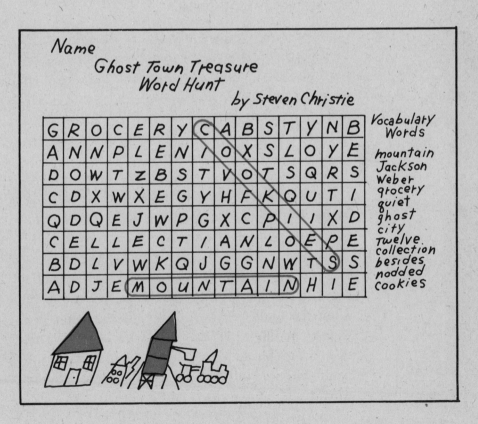

Name

Ghost Town Treasure
Word Hunt
by Steven Christie

G	R	O	C	E	R	Y	C	A	B	S	T	Y	N	B
A	N	N	P	L	E	N	I	O	X	S	L	O	Y	E
D	O	W	T	Z	B	S	T	V	O	T	S	Q	R	S
C	D	X	W	X	E	G	Y	H	F	K	Q	U	T	I
Q	D	Q	E	J	W	P	G	X	C	P	I	I	X	D
C	E	L	L	E	C	T	I	A	N	L	O	E	P	E
B	D	L	V	W	K	Q	J	G	G	N	W	T	S	S
A	D	J	E	M	O	U	N	T	A	I	N	H	I	E

Vocabulary Words

mountain
Jackson
Weber
grocery
quiet
ghost
city
twelve
collection
besides
nodded
cookies

Do-it-yourself crossword puzzles

What happens when you use up the last of the Lucky crossword puzzle pads? If your children clamor for more, try this idea.

Kay Hall creates puzzles based on the book descriptions in the children's *Lucky Book Club News*, and the children make the actual puzzle sheets themselves. "It's really a combination art and reading activity," Mrs. Hall says.

Getting ready

Children who want to participate in the activity must return the entire *Lucky Book Club News* to school. (The order coupon on the back page should *not* be cut out. Be sure to tally the children's orders before beginning the activity.)

First the teacher designs a puzzle grid. To do this, choose seven words from seven different book descriptions — these "key" words are the ones you will use in your crossword. On one side of a sheet of mimeograph paper, draw a grid for the seven words. Then, in the remaining space, mark off boxes where the "Down" and "Across" clues will be inserted and a smaller box labeled "Word Bank." (See illustration.)

Run off copies of the puzzle form and hand one copy to each child who is participating. Make sure scissors and glue are available to all.

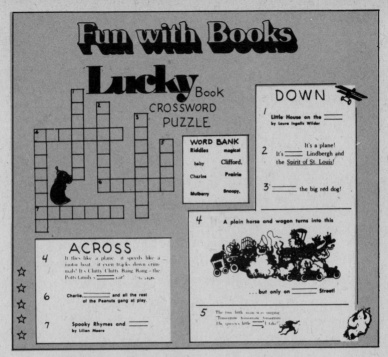

Fun with Books

Lucky Book CROSSWORD PUZZLE

DOWN

1 Little House on the ____
by Laura Ingalls Wilder

2 It's a plane!
It's ____ Lindbergh and
the Spirit of St. Louis!

3 ____ the big red dog!

4 A plain horse and wagon turns into this

... but only on ____ Street!

5 The two little men were singing Tumanzow tomanzow tomanzow The queen's little ____ I take

WORD BANK
Riddles   magical
baby   Clifford,
Charles   Prairie
Mulberry   Snoopy.

ACROSS

4 It flies like a plane, it speeds like a motor boat, it even tracks down criminals! It's Chitty Chitty Bang Bang – the Potts family's ____ car!

6 Charlie, ____ and all the rest of the Peanuts gang at play.

7 Spooky Rhymes and ____
by Lilian Moore

Cutting and pasting

Now each child prepares his own puzzle sheet under your direction. The children first cut out the seven "blurbs" (book descriptions) from which you have chosen your seven key words. Then ask them to cut out the key word from each blurb and glue the seven words in the Word Bank box on their puzzle sheets.

The next (and final) step is for children to glue the seven blurbs minus the key words in the Across and Down boxes in accordance with your directions.

Each child has made his own puzzle! Now the children have the fun of filling in the crossword grid. Like other art projects, the completed puzzles may be displayed on a bulletin board for all to enjoy.

43

Picture puzzles

An effective writing activity uses the mini book covers from the See-Saw or Lucky *Teachers' Guide*.

Cut out the colored pictures of book covers from each month's guide. Let the children choose any one they want, and then paste it onto a piece of lined paper.

The object: to write a sentence about the picture. Children can turn in a piece of creative writing or work on writing a complete sentence, with proper punctuation, capitalization, etc.

Fact or fiction?

"I find the *Lucky Book Club News* a handy teaching aid when trying to help my students differentiate between fact and fiction."

Eileen Bergerson, a second-grade teacher, composes questions that sharpen children's awareness of what is fanciful and what is factual among the books described in the *Lucky News*. She prints four or five questions on an 8½" x 11" ditto master and runs off enough copies for the class. One sheet might include questions like these: *Can you find two stories in your* Lucky News *that could never happen? Write the names of the fanciful books here. Which book tells you true things about one kind of animal? Which book tells you how to do something?*

As they answer these questions, children learn to identify characteristics of factual and fanciful books. And they get valuable practice in reading for specific information.

Jigsaw puzzle bulletin board

Holiday displays gain new excitement with this idea developed by a teacher of first and second grades. As children read new books, they get to put together the pieces of a holiday jigsaw puzzle.

Paint or paste a large holiday symbol on oaktag or other heavy paper. You might choose a witch and cat for October, a Christmas scene for December, and so on. An 18″ x 22″ drawing should be about the right size.

Cut this into puzzle pieces of varying sizes and shapes, from 3″ to 5″ wide and 2″ to 3″ high.

Put the puzzle pieces in a paper bag which you will hang near the bulletin board.

"Usually we start the puzzle off as a group," writes Gayle Kabasa. "I'll read a book to the class and then everyone signs their name to a slip of paper with the title at the top. Someone picks a puzzle piece and pins it, with the list of names, to the bulletin board."

Children can't wait to finish the puzzle. Now, each time a child reads a book on his own, he takes a puzzle piece from the bag, puts the title and his name on a slip of paper, and pins them to the puzzle board.

Sharing the
Joy of Reading

Many children begin to enjoy reading when they have a chance to share books with their classmates.

"Good books make good friends"

Ida May Frischke's third-grade class decides together which books they would like for the classroom collection.

"Each month my Grade 3 class waits anxiously for the *Lucky Book News*. When it arrives, we get into a large circle for a class meeting about the latest paperbacks. Our motto is *Good books make good friends*.

"The children take turns reading the information about each book. We then discuss what books

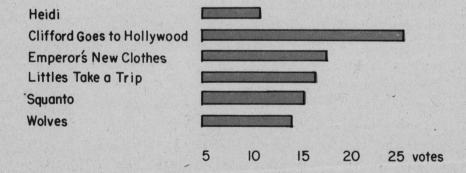

Heidi
Clifford Goes to Hollywood
Emperor's New Clothes
Littles Take a Trip
Squanto
Wolves

5   10   15   20   25 votes

we would like to order and make a graph.

"The most popular book or books are ordered as dividends to be enjoyed by all."

The reading pass

"Two children chuckling over a riddle book, a lilting refrain of 'pickle, pickle, pickle juice,' and the muffled roar of a make-believe dragon, are some of the sounds you would hear as children read in the hall just outside my classroom door," writes Eleanor J. Lapp.

"The reading pass literally opens the door to reading for enjoyment."

This is how the plan works in a busy first- and second-grade classroom:

A small cardboard rectangle with the words READING PASS written on it, is placed in a visible spot at the front of the room. When a child has finished his work, he may take the pass and choose a book from the class collection. Then he stands quietly in front of the room and holds up the book.

Anyone else who is finished with his work may raise his hand. The first child picks a reading partner and, together, they go to two chairs in the hall, where they may read their book aloud.

When the first pair finishes, or when the teacher

wishes them to come back for class, another child may take the pass and choose a reading partner.

Ms. Lapp limits the children to one use of the pass in the morning and one in the afternoon so that many children get the opportunity to use it.

"Children know it is a privilege to read in the hall and the privilege may be suspended for a day if it is misused."

Ms. Lapp concludes, "Children love to read together aloud. Oral expression increases, individual reading differences can be met, and the plan never gets stale because of the great variety in books."

Treat and read time

Friday afternoon is a good time to have "treat and read" time in a primary classroom.

Everyone in class, including the teacher, selects a book to read. The teacher provides a small treat to enjoy — nuts, sunflower seeds, or cookies. Everyone finds a comfortable spot in the room.

When children ask to read together, they are allowed to do so, either using two copies of the same paperback, or taking turns reading softly to one another. Any quiet sharing of a book is appropriate at this time.

Read with a friend

Robin Kavanaugh brings children and paperbacks together in a similar fashion.

She selects multiple copies of paperbacks so that small groups may read a story simultaneously. When a book is of special interest but is difficult for some readers, she provides a cassette tape for them to borrow overnight.

"This read-with-a-friend campaign develops a sense of security and promotes natural and happy discussion," their teacher says. "The shared experience is almost something to give TV-watching a run for its money!"

Paperback powwow

Clea Hollis dubs her class independent reading sessions "paperback powwows."

To encourage reading for pleasure, she lets each child bring a book to class or choose a paperback from the classroom library.

Children read when their assignments are completed or for a short period each day. Then, once a week, the teacher gives time for open discussion — the powwow.

Those who are reading the same book love the chance to compare notes and everyone finds out about books they would like to read.

Supersalespersons

A third-grade teacher tells how to turn a class into supersalespersons *and* superreaders.

Give everyone in class two weeks to find and read a book they enjoy. At the end of the two weeks, explain that each student can have a month to recruit readers for their favorite book.

Every time they convince someone to read their book, they ask that child to complete a form to be returned to the teacher. The supersalesperson is the one turning in the most forms.

The first prize: a free book from the next book club order.

Runners-up each have a chance to pick a dividend book for the classroom.

First- and second-grade classrooms band together for this interest-raising idea.

Each child receives a large sheet of paper which he folds. On the front he prepares a book cover based on the cover of a favorite book; inside the folder he writes his reasons for recommending this book. Each week, post several of these covers in the hall, under the heading READ IT, YOU'LL LIKE IT.

Another special way to share books

After reading a new paperback, each child picks a name from the "name bowl" (a small fish bowl containing the names of all class members on folded strips of paper).

The child must plan a strategy to make the classmate whose name is picked look forward to reading the same book.

They can do this in many ways and are often ingenious in their presentations — question-and-answer sessions, mock TV ads, artwork, or a short summary of the book.

The child whose name is picked may turn down a book and put his name back in the bowl; the first child picks another name.

Children are eager to hear their names called when they have seen a book they would like to read. This exchange continues until all of the children have a new book to enjoy.

Display books that a number of children have read and enjoyed with the children's comments about them.

Favorite-book fan clubs

"When the class becomes interested in a specific Lucky character, such as Clifford the big red dog, or a favorite author, such as Arnold Lobel, we form a book club," writes Molly Adams, a second-grade teacher.

Mrs. Adams has a collection of the Clifford books that she has received as free dividends over the years. To start the Clifford Book Club, she chose four titles and placed the books in a reading corner. She then made up a short and easy membership test with questions about each of the books on display.

Any Clifford fan who reads all of the books is eligible to take the test. If the child passes — Mrs. Adams sets a limit to the number of questions that can be missed — the child's name goes up on a big poster that is hung on the door, and he receives a membership card. For extra fun, the card for the Clifford Book Club is in the shape of a dog.

If a child fails the test, he is encouraged to take it again after re-reading the books. "The idea of these clubs is not to be exclusive," Mrs. Adams notes, "but for the child to comprehend what he is reading. Children really enjoy this activity."

Getting Parents Involved

An exchange of books between classroom and home gives parents a chance to see how their children are reading. Parents enjoy knowing what interests their children and they appreciate the chance to become involved in the learning process.

A kindergarten library

Even before children can read, they benefit from a familiarity with books. One kindergarten teacher runs a lending library in her own classroom.

Each month she selects about 30 books for a book table — the books come from the school library, book club purchases, and her own personal collection.

Every child chooses a book and takes it home in a large manila envelope provided by the teacher. Parents write the title of the book on the envelope, and over a period of time there will be a record of the books a child has read or listened to.

Parents read to their children every day — many enjoy the books as much as the children do!

"Just hopping to tell you . . ."

One first-grade teacher puts a box of mimeographed slips for a parent to fill out next to the books that go home. Boys and girls take a slip with each book that is checked out; later they return the books with the slips.

"Make plenty of these!" advises Leona Stacy.

Parents can read the books to their children or listen to the children read them aloud. Either way, the goal is to motivate interest in books and get parents involved.

Multi-purpose book bags

Write each child's name and address on a piece of paper; staple these labels onto plastic bags or Baggies. Use these to transport books and notes home to the parents.

During the school year, where this system has been used, not one paperback was lost permanently from the class library. Book bags were found on buses, in playgrounds, and even in a few snowbanks, but were returned eventually, and in good condition!

Parents began to look for the book bags and commented that it was helpful to have a book on hand when a child complained of nothing to do.

Parents' night

Put out a selection of paperbacks on parents' visiting nights — on desk tops or along the blackboard. If parents' interest is aroused, they will encourage their children. Quite often, books are borrowed then and there to share with the children at home.

An End-of-the-Year Festival

Plan a festive break from end-of-the-year testing around one or more of the following ideas.

A balloon book party

To end the school year with a bang, have a balloon party.

Choose books (Lucky paperbacks and/or hardcovers) from your classroom library and divide them into groups according to reading levels. Place the bunches of books in various parts of the room and number each station.

Now you will need balloons (one for each child) and small strips of paper for each balloon. Print the number of a group on each strip of paper and insert the strip into a balloon. Blow up the balloon, and with a felt-tipped pen print the name of each child on a balloon that will guide him to a book he can read.

The balloons are handed out and at the count of three, each child breaks his balloon. The child finds the slip of paper and goes to the appropriate station where he selects his book for silent reading. Later, the children may draw pictures to show when telling each other about the book.

School-wide read-a-thon

The month of May brings the excitement of a reading marathon to one elementary school.

All classes are divided into three teams, with each team including an equal number of first-, second-, third-, and fourth-grade children. Each team is assigned a team color.

The read-a-thon takes on a special theme such as "Jogging for Books."

Once the race is on, each child has an opportunity to read a book a day to advance the team. Parents have a part in the contest too: for each book a child reads, parents must sign a note verifying that the book has been read.

When the classroom teacher receives a parent's note, she gives the child a paper token to deposit in the team's box, which is centrally located in the school. These tokens tie in with the theme — they might be in the shape of a footprint for this race; on it the child prints his name, room number, and the title of the book he read. The tokens and the team box are color-coded in that team's color.

The children's tokens are taped up along the corridors at the end of each day, wending their way along the hallways. Each team is placed in its own track so that all can follow the progress to the finish line.

"For the past three years, the read-a-thon has generated total school involvement," writes Jan

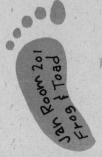

Merchant. "Children can be heard daily walking down the hall saying, 'I read that book. It's great!' or 'Which books have you read this week?'

"Our contest usually runs about three weeks and totals about 2,600 books read. At the conclusion, an assembly is held. Each team receives recognition for its efforts. Whether a team wins or loses, girls and boys enjoy the competition and so do their families."

Pack a summer book box

The last week of school is very exciting for one group of second-graders who are having difficulty mastering reading skills. This is the week they pack their book boxes to take home over summer vacation.

Mrs. Joy Hanson, a media specialist, has the girls and boys select 10 books from paperbacks purchased in advance by the school.

The whole class votes on which paperback each child will get as a reward for returning the books next year, along with mini book-report forms. One

New Words

Title _____

Have a whale of a time this summer. READ! READ! READ!

year Mrs. Hanson's class voted for *The Littles;* other years, the choices for reward books were *Curious George* and *Amelia Bedelia.*

A letter to parents and mini book-report forms are included in the book box (see below).

Because of the success of the book boxes in Mrs. Hanson's school, where 85% of the second-graders read and returned their books, first-graders were later included in the project.

Dear Parents,

    Will you help us perform an experiment? It has been our experience that children often forget their reading skills over the summer. So, we are sending 10 books home with your child in the hope that he will read them and keep in practice.

    The sheets with the whales on them are included so that your child will write down new words and also put down a few sentences about the book. Six filled whales turned in next fall will result in a reward.

    Help your child have a whale of a time this summer and encourage him to read.

            Sincerely,

            Joy Hanson, Media Specialist

P.S. Return books first week of school in the fall.

Recycling paperbacks — a spring book fair

This book fair is different in that no one needs any money and everyone can trade old books for new ones.

Shortly before the close of school, a week is designated "Book Fair Week." The first three days are "selling" days, when children bring in paperbacks they wish to "recycle." They exchange their books for cardboard tokens equal to the original purchase price of the book.

The books are set out on long tables and grouped by approximate level of difficulty.

Thursday and Friday are "buying" days. Children turn in their tokens for their new books.

Use class library time for this activity, and have the children do their buying in several stages so that early buyers do not take all the popular books at once.

The great paperback award show

Children are familiar with award shows for movies, television, and sports — now they can have their own award presentation for paperbacks. This idea works well with very experienced and able readers.

Start with a planning session in which the class works together to list categories for the awards: best books in mystery, science, humor, and folk tales, for example. Other categories might be best author, best artist, favorite character from a book.

You may want to work with each student individually to review book reports and other records of books they have read during the year. Then turn over the rest of the work to committees to plan the show.

One group designs the voting ballots; another will present the "nominees" to the class; another plans "acceptance" speeches that will explain why the book won the award. A fourth committee oversees stage props and publicity for the show. Parents and other children in the same grade or next lower grade will make an enthusiastic audience.

As the production is being planned, keep track of nominated books on a large bulletin board. Don't forget to post the closing date for all ballots.

The Great Paperback Award Show will generate lasting enthusiasm for books. Children learn the importance of working together to make this special event a huge success.

Teachers who contributed to this book

Molly Adams, *Central School, Plainfield, Illinois.*

Susan Anderson Hooper, *Happy Valley School, Portland, Oregon.*

Sister Antoninus, O.P., *Overbrook School, Nashville, Tennessee.*

Inez Barry, *Lincoln School, Mt. Pleasant, Iowa.*

Eileen Bergerson, *Wilmot Public Schools, Wilmot, South Dakota.*

Enid Bjarnson, *Woodstock School, Salt Lake City, Utah.*

Lillie J. Brown, *Sawtooth Elementary School, Twin Falls, Idaho.*

Zola Brown, *Sunset Beach Christian School, Haleiwa, Hawaii.*

Beverly Clayton, *Hibriten Extended School Day, Lenoir, North Carolina.*

Janice N. Crouthamel, *Alfarath School, Huntingdon, Pennsylvania.*

Joyce Dahlquist, *Western Elementary School, Russiaville, Indiana.*

Melinda Diamond, *Trace Elementary School, San Jose, California.*

Barbara Eberhard, *Park School, Sturgis, Michigan.*

Ida May Frischke, *John Wilson Elementary School, Innisfail, Canada.*

Susan Gambs, *Thorson School, Crystal, Minnesota.*

Gail Greenberg, *James Fenimore Cooper School, Cherry Hill, New Jersey.*

Kay Hall, *Grape Greek School, San Angelo, Texas.*

Joy Hanson, *Cook Elementary School, Midland, Michigan.*

Mary Hogan, *Fort Meadow School, Westfield, Massachusetts.*

Clea P. Hollis, *Richland School District, Johnstown, Pennsylvania.*

Frances S. Husdale, *Linden Elementary School, Sheridan, Wyoming.*

Judy Jones, *Springhill Elementary, Hope, Arkansas.*

Gayle Kabasa, *St. Louis School, Washburn, Wisconsin.*

Robin Kavanaugh, *St. John Bosco Primary School, Australia.*

Eleanor J. Lapp, *Phelps School, Phelps, Wisconsin.*

Caroline Hartmann Levine, *Kenton School, Aurora, Colorado.*

Wilhelmina Berger Lewis, *Hatfield Elementary, Hatfield, Pennsylvania.*

Carolyn London, *Trinity School, Los Angeles, California.*

Rebecca Mallet, *Gilchrist Elementary School, Gilchrist, Oregon.*

Lois Marquardt, *Douglas MacArthur School, Cleveland, Ohio.*

Lois Martin, *St. Joseph's School, Mishawaka, Indiana.*

George G. McLaughlin, *Joshua Howard School, Dearborn, Michigan.*

Jan Merchant, *Brooks Hill School, Fairport, New York.*

Maude C. Mueller, *Coulterville Public School, Coulterville, Illinois.*

Garry Munday, *Gladstone Public School, Gladstone, Australia.*

Mary Murphy, *Memorial School, Natick, Massachusetts.*

Paulette O'Doherty, *California Avenue School, Uniondale, New York.*

Susan Orf, *Ascension School, St. Louis, Missouri.*

Phyllis O'Sullivan, *P.S. 53, Staten Island, New York.*

Ann Pinto, *Central School, Hampstead, New Hampshire.*

Mary Anne Piskulich, *Reavis Primary Center, Affton, Missouri.*

Eleanor J. Rahman, *Hatchery Hill School, Hackettstown, New Jersey.*

Peg Reno, *Harry McGinnis Middle School, Buena Vista, Colorado.*

Nina Rohm, *Cromwell Elementary School, Cromwell, Indiana.*

Joann Schmitt, *St. Jude School, Green Bay, Wisconsin.*

Ann Scott, *Hamilton College School, Australia.*

Leona Stacy, *Lewis Grade School, Lewis, Kansas.*

Jean Swenson, *Washington School, Marshfield, Wisconsin.*

Fern Thompson, *Madison School, Mason City, Iowa.*

Amy Zehm, *Lynnvale School, White Mills, Kentucky.*